Photograph by Olwen Way

Robert Way is an antiquarian book-seller in Newmarket. He is married, with five children and two grand-children. After reading for a degree in classics and rural economy at Cambridge he spent a long period farming and breeding thoroughbred horses, before taking up bookselling. He has now handed the business over to his son in order that he may devote himself to travelling widely in search of books.

THE GARDEN
OF THE BELOVED

No disciple is above his Master but everyone when he is perfected is as his Master.

Luke 6:40.

Robert Way

The
Garden of the
Beloved

illustrations by
Laszlo Kubinyi

Sheldon Press
London

To my grandchildren,
James and Katherine,
in hopes that they too may learn
the art of loving.

First published in the USA in 1975 by
Doubleday & Company Inc.

First published in Great Britain in 1975 by
Sheldon Press, Marylebone Road, London NW1 4DU

Printed in Great Britain by
Wood Westworth & Co. Ltd., St. Helens, Merseyside.

ISBN 0 85969 061 X

Contents

I beheld, thinking what manner of labor it might be that the servant should do. And then I understood that he should do the greatest labor and the hardest travail, that is, he should be a gardener. Delve and dyke, toil and sweat and turn the earth upside down and seek deepness and water the plants in time, and in this he should continue his travail and make sweet floods run and noble and plenteous fruits to spring which he should bring before the Lord and serve him therewith to his desire.

Julian of Norwich: *Revelations of Divine Love*

The rapturous nightingale sings
Wooing the rose
In the midst of the Garden newborn
But only the gardener knows
Of the labor that brings
To the Garden its beauty; he toiled all day in the heat
And his feet
Have been wounded by many a thorn.

The Diwan of Zeb-un-Nissa, translated by
Magan Lal and J. D. Westbrook.
[By permission of John Murray (publishers) Ltd.]

I ⁂ *The Apprenticing of the Disciple*

The Lover was working in the Garden which the Beloved had given to him. All around him the Garden shone
with a glorious radiance of color, and sweet scents rose
like incense. For the Lover had planted in the Garden
beautiful flowers of every kind and fragrant herbs and all
such plants as are fair to look upon or are beneficial to
men. All this he planted for the pleasure of the Beloved,
and he tended it for the love he bore the Beloved, and as
he worked he sang the words of Solomon which he sang in
his garden.

"Awake, O North wind, and come, thou South
Blow upon my garden that spices may flow out
Let my Beloved come into his garden
and eat of his precious fruits."

While he thus sang and worked, there came into the Garden a young man dressed in rich clothes who wore at his side a gilded rapier, set with jewels, yet upon the handsome face of the man was an expression of sorrow and great yearning. He approached the Lover, who was clothed only in his coarse gardener's robe, and bowing humbly before him said to him:

"Sir, I have heard that you are a master craftsman in the art of Love and I desire beyond all things to become proficient in this art. I wondered if perhaps of your charity, you would take as an apprentice one as ignorant and unskilled as myself. Whatever apprentice fee is due to you for this I will gladly pay it, for I am rich as men count wealth."

The Lover ceased from the digging in which he was engaged and looked at the man long and searchingly, then since he was pleased with what he saw he answered, "Stranger, for myself I should desire nothing if you should become apprentice under me, for it is reward enough for me and more than enough that I should be able to perform any task which is pleasing to the Beloved or would make others love Him more. But to the Beloved you would have to pay a fee so high that almost all who seek this service are offended at it."

"Then," answered the stranger, "tell me, I beg you, what this great fee is, for so greatly do I desire to learn to love, that however high it is I will gladly pay it."

"The fee," replied the Lover, "is no less than this, that you give everything that you have and everything that you are so that you have nothing left that is your own, but only hold all things for the sake of the Beloved, for if you hold back anything at all you can never truly know the love of the Beloved. Not that He will love you any the less, for He already loves you to the full, but because your perception will be so clouded by that which you possess that in your blindness you will never see the love of the Beloved."

"If," asked the stranger, "I pay this great price, tell me, I pray you, what I shall gain?"

Then answered the Lover, "When you have learned with much labor all the mysteries of the art of Love, then when you have suffered much, you will gain at last the knowledge of the love of the Beloved."

Thereupon the stranger, for his soul greatly longed for the love of the Beloved, gladly paid the whole fee and stripped off the rich robes he was wearing which men call Knowledge and Pride and assumed the coarse gardener's habit, Humility, such as the Lover himself wore, and he threw away the jeweled rapier which he was carrying which men call Learning, and took in its place a gardener's spade the name of which is Seeking.

As he did this it seemed that the day which had been gray and cloudy became suddenly glorious and bright as though the sun had suddenly broken through the clouds.

So the Lover received the stranger and he became his disciple and he and the Lover worked to make the Garden beautiful for the sake of the Beloved.

II ❧ *The Disciple and the Caterpillars*

So it was that the Disciple passed his days working in the Garden of the Beloved and listening to the instruction of the Lover.

Now the Garden was full of birds with beautiful plumage which sang continually the praise of the Beloved, and of brightly colored butterflies which played about the flowers so that the bushes seemed to blaze with a splendor not their own.

One day as the Disciple was passing through the Garden, he noticed that the leaves of certain plants were ragged and full of holes. Then looking more closely he saw there were on them many small caterpillars, dung-colored and covered with hideous hairs, which even as he looked were eating the leaves of the plants.

When he saw this it seemed to him that they were doing great harm to the Garden of the Beloved, so he plucked them one by one from the plants and crushed them beneath his heel.

At that moment the Lover came through the Garden and when he saw what the Disciple was doing, he wept, yet he spoke gently to the Disciple and said, "I know that you have acted through ignorance and with a good heart in doing this, yet in doing it you have greatly hurt the beauty of the Garden of the Beloved."

The Disciple when he heard this was amazed and very sorrowful.

The Lover then showed the Disciple another plant where he saw caterpillars enveloping themselves in cocoons of silk. There were many cocoons on the stems of the leaves and even as he watched, one split and from it came a butterfly with wings like the rainbow. Then he perceived how in his ignorance he had hurt the Garden of the Beloved.

III ❦ *The Disciple and the Worms*

One day, the Lover took the Disciple and told him to dig up a patch of waste ground. When the Lover told him to do this the Disciple was very glad for usually the Lover kept to himself all such hard tasks, and therefore he dug zealously and deep and as he dug he turned up many loathsome worms, slimy and obscene. These, since his heart had grown more gentle than when first he entered the Garden, he collected carefully together in a sack although he much disliked touching them, and carrying them to the edge of the Garden put them beyond its bounds, for it seemed to him intolerable that any such hideous things should deface the glory of the Garden of the Beloved.

So when the time came for planting the Garden they sowed seed throughout the Garden where they had dug it, and in due season lovely flowers and green herbs sprung up everywhere save only the plot which the Disciple had dug. This remained bare and barren.

When the Disciple saw this he was very sad and going to the Lover asked him saying, "Sir, tell me, I pray you, is it my sins that have rendered the plot which I dug barren and yielding no fruit or beauty to the Beloved?"

The Lover answered, "Tell me carefully all that you did when you dug this plot."

To which the Disciple replied, "I put my spade deep into the earth for I was glad of hard toil in the service of the Beloved. Then I turned over the earth with my spade and in it were many loathsome worms. These, much as I disliked touching them, I placed in a sack and carried outside the boundary of the Garden. For I desired to move such ugliness from the Garden of the Beloved."

Then said the Lover, "These creatures which seemed to you so loathsome are fellow workers with us in the service of the Beloved, for burrowing in the earth they allow air to get to the roots of the plants and they swallow and digest the earth so that the plants can draw nourishment from it, and without their help no plant can grow. So you see indeed these creatures which seem to us so loathsome are in truth more profitable servants to the Beloved than we are ourselves."

The Disciple then asked, "How can I repair this great damage which in my ignorance I have done to the Garden?"

The Lover replied, "Go out of the Garden to the place where you put the worms and dig there so that you may find these or other worms which you can bring back to the plot to work for the glory of the Garden of the Beloved."

The Disciple went out of the Garden though he much disliked leaving it even for so short a time and dug and took up the worms and lifting them very lovingly and with great reverence brought them to the barren plot which thereafter was barren no more.

IV ❧ *The Disciple and the Nightingale*

Now as has already been written there were in the Garden many beautiful birds and their voices mingled together so that no one might ever perceive from which bird each song came, yet the whole melody was of indescribable sweetness.

Among all these birds there was only one which had no beauty. It was small and brown and looked like a pebble in a casket of jewels. So it seemed to the Disciple like a wedding guest who had put on no wedding garment for the sake of the Beloved. Therefore he was very angry for the Beloved's sake and drove the bird from the Garden.

But no sooner had it flown out than, although all the other birds still sang melodiously, the song of the Garden seemed to have lost its sweetness and the lovely roses in the Garden dropped their heads and began to die.

At once the Lover came out and asked the Disciple what had become of the brown bird.

The Disciple was amazed and told the Lover all that had happened.

Whereon the Lover went swiftly out of the Garden and called the brown bird which came flying and perched on his shoulder. So he brought it into the Garden again and it sang joyously because it had returned to the Garden. Thereupon the whole Garden was filled with melody and the roses lifted their heads again.

Then the Disciple asked the Lover, "Sir, please tell me what bird this is and how did you perceive at once that it was absent from the Garden?"

The Lover replied, "It is called the nightingale and by as much as its plumage is less beautiful than that of the other birds, by that much its voice is sweeter and louder than all of theirs, so that it fills all the Garden with melody, and so beautiful is its song that when the roses no longer hear it they drop their heads."

So the Disciple perceived that each thing has its own gifts to bring to the service of the Beloved.

v ❧ *The Disciple and*
the Strange Bird

On another day the Disciple saw outside the Garden a
bird with plumage so bright that it seemed to outshine all
the splendid birds of the Garden. When he saw it the
Disciple thought that so beautiful a bird should be in the
Garden for the pleasure of the Beloved. So going out of
the Garden with much difficulty he caught the bird and
though it tried hard to escape took it into the Garden and
putting it on a tree went about his appointed tasks. But
no sooner had the Disciple departed than the bird flew
from the tree and began to tear off the flowers of the

Garden and scatter the fruits and it tore the wings off the butterflies and attacked the birds that were in the Garden and tore out their bright feathers and injured many.

When the Disciple returned and saw the havoc which had been wrought in the Garden, he was very angry, and after a long chase caught the bird and put his hand on its head to slay it although its beak pierced his finger to the bone. But at that moment he heard the voice of the Lover, who said, "My son, do not kill that bird but turn it out of the Garden, for the time will yet come when it will be serviceable to the Beloved although as yet it knows nothing of Love. Do not blame the bird, for the fault is yours for you brought it into the Garden although it was unwilling."

When he heard this the Disciple wept and where his tears fell the flowers bloomed anew and the hurts of the birds were healed.

So the Disciple again perceived how the appearance of things may deceive.

VI ❧ *The Disciple and the Bats*

One day the Disciple came to the Lover and said, "Sir, I begin to see that each thing in the Garden works for the glory of the Garden of the Beloved, yet there is in the uttermost part of the Garden a most malodorous cave where live black bats of hideous aspect. These have no beauty to please the Beloved nor voice to praise Him, nor do they seem to do any service in the Garden of the Beloved. Tell me, Sir, I beg you, how are these pleasing to the Beloved?"

The Lover smiled, for he understood that the Disciple

was growing in his perception of the Beloved, and he answered, "My son, these strange creatures most certainly do great service in the Garden of the Beloved, for as they wheel overhead in the night sky they destroy many noxious insects which would do great harm in the Garden, and as they fly they cry continually the praises of the Beloved but their voices are pitched so high that our ears are not attuned to hear them. Furthermore, do as I say and you will see another great service which they do for the Garden of the Beloved. Go into the cave and bring out what you find on the floor of the cave and put it on one of the beds in the Garden."

The Disciple did as he was told although he greatly disliked entering the cave because it was evil-smelling beyond anything that he had encountered in his life, for he was gently bred, yet he did not hesitate to carry out the Lover's orders and spread on one of the beds of the Garden the gray slime which he had lifted from the floor of the cave, for although he could not see how this would be pleasing to the Beloved yet he well knew the Wisdom of the Lover.

From that bed sprung up flowers taller and more beautiful than all the flowers in the Garden.

So he saw how man in his ignorance often fails to perceive services of other creatures of the Beloved.

And thereafter he often brought from the cave the bats' offering to the Beloved.

VII ❧ *The Disciple and*
the Boulder

For a long time after the Disciple came into the Garden of the Beloved, the Lover gave him light tasks about the Garden, until at last the Disciple, being very zealous to do some great task for the Beloved, chafed against the lightness of his toil. So he said to the Lover, "Sir, please give me some heavier work that I can do for the Beloved, for I greatly wish to do Him greater service."

The Lover thereon took him to a distant part of the Garden where there was a great boulder and said to him, "This boulder would fit well in the rock garden of the

Beloved. If you want a heavy task, move the boulder there."

The Disciple was amazed, for it seemed to him that the boulder was too big for any man to move, nevertheless he was ashamed not to attempt the task he had been allotted. So when the Lover departed he struggled throughout the whole day to move the boulder and actually did with extreme exertion move it a few inches. Toward evening, when he was utterly exhausted, the Lover came to him and easily lifting the boulder in his arms carried it to the rock garden. The Disciple was astonished and said to the Lover, "Sir, please tell me the meaning of this task and whence your marvelous strength comes."

The Lover replied, "My muscles like my faith have become strong little by little by carrying out my daily tasks in the Garden, but you by demanding a task for which you are not yet fitted have wasted a whole day when you might have been usefully serving the Beloved by weeding his Garden."

So the Disciple saw that a man must first undertake little acts of love and only as his skill and strength increase through doing these undertake greater.

VIII ❧ The Disciple and the Crown of Thorns

One day after the Disciple had been working in the Garden for a long time he came to the Lover and said, "Sir, I want to experience suffering for the Beloved's sake."

The Lover answered, "I often hear you complaining that thorns tear your arms and nettles sting your face and the spade galls your hands; what is this if it is not suffering for the Beloved's sake?"

"These," the Disciple replied, "are only common accidents that happen to all gardeners. I would feel the suffering that befalls the Lovers of the Beloved."

The Lover said nothing but looked sadly at him and led him to a walled part of the Garden where he had never been before. In the middle of the enclosure stood a cross. When the Disciple saw it he was overcome with terror and trembled violently, but the Lover took him by the arm and leading him to the foot of the cross said, "This is the cross of the Beloved and on it all His Lovers must suffer."

Then an anguish of fear fell on the Disciple and he could not speak and his limbs would barely support him. The Lover took up a circlet of cruel thorns and placed it gently on the Disciple's head. As soon as the thorns touched his flesh the Disciple felt about his brow an agony of torment as if all the pain in the world had come together in that one place. In his terror and pain he fainted and knew no more. When he revived he was lying on the soft grass of the outer Garden and the Lover sat beside him regarding him with pity. Then for the first time the Disciple saw that there were scars on the Lover's hands and feet and on his brows and the tunic under his armpits was dyed with a red dye.

"My son," said the Lover, "how when you could not bear joyously for the Beloved's sake the little common hurts of His Garden could you hope to bear the torments of the Lovers of the Beloved? Truly the crown was laid so lightly on your brow that not a thorn pierced the skin."

So the Disciple saw that the Beloved allows to each Lover only such suffering as he is able to bear and joyfully thereafter bore the small hurts of the Garden.

IX ❧ *The Comforting
of the Disciple*

Now the Beloved often came into the Garden both because of the great joy He had in the Garden and because
of the great love He bore the Lover and the Disciple.
Often He talked with the Lover, but the Disciple because
he was not yet perfected in Love could neither hear nor
see the Beloved, though he often felt a strange joy, he did
not know why. Therefore he was sorrowful, for it seemed
to him that on account of his sins he would never find the
Beloved. So weeping he came to the Lover and said, "Sir,
I know that I am a very sinful man and I much fear that

though I search all my life yet on account of my sins I shall never find the Beloved."

In reply the Lover smiled gently and said, "My son, when you first came into the Garden do you remember what sort of day it was?"

"Yes," said the Disciple, "I remember it. It was dark and gloomy as if no sunlight ever entered the Garden."

"When you began to strip off your rich robes," the Lover asked, "what happened to the day?"

"It seemed," said the Disciple, "as if the sun had suddenly broken through the clouds and the whole Garden shone with glorious and celestial light: such light as shines daily in the Garden."

The Lover replied, "Know that the Beloved Himself is the light of the Garden, so that when you began searching for the Beloved even then you found Him, for how can any know the desire to search for the Beloved if He had not already without his knowing revealed Himself to him."

So the Disciple was greatly comforted by knowing that although he could not see or hear Him he had already found the Beloved, and he labored the more joyously to do the service of the Beloved.

x 🐒 *The Beautiful*

Said the Disciple to the Lover, "Sir, before I left the world I heard certain men who were held in high esteem and thought to know the will of the Beloved say that those who loved the Beautiful did not love the Beloved but loved idols, yet in the Garden of the Beloved we are ever striving to create beauty for the pleasure of the Beloved. Were they then speaking the truth?"

The Lover answered, "Those who said this had never glimpsed the form of the Beloved nor ever truly sought Him, for all beauty is but the reflection of the beauty of the Beloved, although seen very dimly as in a dark and faulty mirror, even as all goodness is a dim reflection of the goodness of the Beloved. So it is that those who love beauty and goodness recognize dimly in them the form of the Beloved and though often in ignorance those who are seeking the Beautiful and the Good are seeking after the Beloved."

XI 🦋 *The Moths*

One evening as the Lover and the Disciple were sitting by the light of a candle a moth flew around the candle and seemed to warm itself in the flame. Seeing this the Disciple said, "Sir, surely this moth is like a Lover who warms himself in the love of the Beloved."

"No, my son," said the Lover. "This is like an unworthy seeker who although he perceives the love of the Beloved yet for fear that he should lose that which he has does not approach near the heat of His love."

A little later after this moth had flown away, another

moth came which flew so near the flame that its wings were scorched and all the lovely colors burned off them, after which it flew out into the darkness.

Then the Disciple said, "Sir, surely this moth must be like the true Lover of the Beloved, for see, by reason of the great love which it bore the flame, its wings are scorched and all its lovely colors departed."

"Not so," said the Lover. "This moth is like a timorous Lover who although he has tasted the joy of the Beloved yet when he feels the first searing pains of love flees from the flame and forsakes the Beloved."

Then another moth flew in, which as soon as it perceived the candle did not flutter around it as the others had done but flew straight to it and throwing itself into the flame was utterly immolated, becoming one with the flame itself.

"See," said the Lover, "like this is the true Lover of the Beloved, for thinking of nothing else he throws himself utterly into the burning love of the Beloved."

XII 🎜 *The Overladen*
Packhorse

One day there came by the Garden a man driving a pack-horse and it was thin and weak with hunger and its back was badly galled by the pack saddle and its load was so heavy that although its master beat it continually with a great stick it moved forward very slowly. When the Lover saw this he went out of the Garden and said to the man, "Brother, why do you keep on beating your poor pack-horse? Can you not see that it is through weakness and heaviness of his load that he cannot make a better pace?"

The man replied, "Stranger, have no pity on this horse,

for he is an evil beast. Once I used to look after him well, giving him all the corn he could eat and only working him lightly and grooming him each day and resting him for the slightest hurt, yet he became wild and unmanageable and when I put any burden on him he reared up and broke his girths and he hurt me badly both by throwing me when I tried to ride him and striking at me with his forefeet. And if he saw a mare no man could hold him but he would break loose and do a great deal of harm. So I swore that I would overcome his wildness and wantonness with little food and heavy loads and much beating, but now that I have tamed him he has become sullen and despite all my blows he goes so slowly that I fear that I shall be late for the market and lose all the trouble I had making the journey."

Then said the Lover, "Friend, you have not acted wisely in this, for it is not surprising that when he received a great deal of corn and spent his time in idleness he got out of hand through the overindulgence of his flesh, but now it is you yourself who are the loser, for through starvation and neglect he has become too weak to carry the heavy burden you have put on him. Take my advice then; leave half your load in my care and go with the other half to the market so that you may not be too late and lose all your labor."

The man did as the Lover advised and the packhorse, feeling its load so much lightened, made good pace to the market so that the merchant arrived just in time to sell the goods he had with him at a good profit. Then he returned to the Garden to collect the things which he had left with the Lover and said to the Lover, "Thank you very much for your good advice, for had I taken the whole load I would not have reached the market in time and would have lost all the fruits of my labor."

Then said the Lover, "Let me give you this further advice: take your horse home and feed him well, not on rich oats but on good plain hay and grass—put salve on his galls and work him each day not with excessive tasks but with work fitted to his strength, but don't let him be idle. Do not keep beating your horse as you have been doing, for if you beat him when he goes well you have no remedy left for when he goes badly."

The merchant promised he would do as the Lover advised. He went home and kept his promise and many times after that the Lover and the Disciple saw the man lead the horse past the Garden. Soon the horse was fat and in good condition, yet since his food was not overrich and he was not left in idleness he did not get out of hand. Soon he regained his strength and was able to bear loads far greater than those he had carried when first he passed the Garden, but he did not find them too heavy and made good pace to the market.

The Lover said to the Disciple, "Do you see a parable in this?"

The Disciple answered, "No Sir, please explain it to me."

"The packhorse," said the Lover, "is like our body which bears loads of duties and good deeds for the soul its master; but if the body is overindulged in sensual pleasures and idleness it becomes wanton and unmanageable. On account of this many who would serve the Beloved make the contrary mistake and afflict and starve their bodies, bringing them into subjection indeed but at the same time making them incapable of serving their masters and bearing a full burden of good deeds to the Beloved, for as you have seen it is labor in vain to load a packhorse beyond its strength. Therefore give to the packhorse—your body—what is needed for its sustenance but do not over-indulge it; keep it employed but do not afflict it unnecessarily, for remember that it too is a servant of the Beloved."

XIII ❧ *The Proud Minister*

One day there came into the Garden a man in torn clothes badly bruised and cut, who said to the Lover, "In the name of the Beloved I demand your help."

So the Lover and the Disciple led him in and dressed his wounds and prepared the best of the vegetables from the Garden for him to eat. When his wounds had been dressed and he had eaten and rested the Lover asked him how he had fallen into this plight, to which the man replied, "I was Minister of the Beloved in a city near this place, where I preached His gospel and expounded His doctrine to the people. I pointed out to them how their sins had made them wholly hateful to the Beloved and how therefore they were utterly beyond the range of His love and He would condemn them to eternal torments, whereon some fell into despair and wept bitterly but many were angry. One day the magistrates called me before them and begged me to leave the city and preach elsewhere for they said I had made many people so angry and desperate that they feared there might be a riot and they might not be able to protect me but that I might suffer some injury. I, however, very zealous for the Beloved and believing that the magistrates only feared that their own sins might be proclaimed, preached the more vehemently, denounced the magistrates and made it abundantly clear that the whole wicked city was foredoomed to eternal punishment by the just provision of the Beloved. Whereon a mob, stirred up no doubt by the corrupt and venal magistrates, fell upon me with sticks and stones, nearly killing me and driving me out of the city in the state in which I came to you."

"My friend," said the Lover, "this was not a good deed of yours, for besides denying the unfathomable compassion of the Beloved, you have by your obstinacy caused these people to commit a grievous sin, and this cannot be pleasing to the Beloved, that through you who profess to be His minister the people should become worse. Surely you remember that He Himself said, 'If they persecute you in one city flee to another.'"

Therefore the man was very angry, and cursing the Lover, said, "I see that I have had a very false report of you and I do not believe that you are a servant of the Beloved at all. When I came to you so injured for the Beloved's sake you set before me only herbs and fruits although the garden is full of birds which you could have killed to make me a worthy meal. I shall proclaim everywhere that you are no true servant of the Beloved but a mere falterer who dares not suffer in the cause of the Beloved. Be sure that you are foreordained to eternal torments who suffer nothing here."

For the man was so blinded by his own pride that he could not perceive the scars on the hands and feet and the brows of the Lover nor how the cloth beneath the armpits of his tunic was dyed with a red dye. So he went out of the Garden cursing and shouting.

But the Lover looked sad and said, "A man like this does much harm to the cause of the Beloved, for by thus speaking falsely about the Beloved he may bring men to fear Him but none to love Him, and by love alone can any man approach the Beloved."

XIV 🌿 *The Death of the Lover*

For many, many years the Disciple worked in the Garden of the Beloved and learned the wisdom of Love from the Lover. Although he still had never actually seen the Beloved nor heard His voice, yet whenever the Beloved visited the Garden he beheld the wondrous light of Him and knew the ineffable joy of His presence.

Now the Lover had grown old and his eyes became dim from beholding the splendor of the Beloved and his body was almost consumed by the fire of his love, yet for the joy he had in the service of the Beloved he still did all the work that he was able in the Garden but as his powers failed more and more work of the Garden fell to the lot of the Disciple, whose frame had become so inured to toil and his strength so increased that he was able to perform all the tasks and had great joy in thus serving the Beloved.

One day the Lover called the Disciple and said, "Rejoice with me, my son, for today I go to the Beloved."

The Disciple was sorry when he heard that the Lover was going to leave him, yet he rejoiced at the Lover's happiness because he was going to the Beloved.

Then the Lover said, "Look after the Garden well for the Beloved's sake, but I know that you will do this, and rejoice at the toils and torments with which the Beloved will try you, for I think that your hour is near."

After saying this the Lover lay down to rest and on his lips was a smile of peace passing human understanding. So he went to the Beloved whose faithful Lover he was.

The Disciple wept for the love which he bore the Lover. He was ashamed of these selfish tears which he shed at the happiness of the Lover and taking up the body of the Lover, although it was but an empty shell, he buried it in the most beautiful part of the Garden, and looked after the Garden with even more care than before both for the love he bore the Lover and the love he bore the Beloved. From the words of the Lover he had great hope that he too would soon go to the Beloved, but in this he was mistaken.

XV ❧ *The Passion*
of the Disciple

Not long after the death of the Lover, while the Disciple was diligently weeding the Garden of the Beloved he heard a knock on the gate and found a man standing there dressed in a silk robe and accompanied by seven young men but little less finely dressed than himself. In his hand he bore a deed sealed as it seemed with the seal of the Beloved whereby he who bore it was appointed to take charge of the Garden of the Beloved and choose such assistants as he might think fit. The Disciple examined the deed and the seal of the Beloved carefully and both of them seemed to him to be in order, nor did he think it a strange or grievous thing that the Beloved should appoint another over him in the Garden since he himself had not sufficient virtue to hear the Beloved or see His face, and although it is true that a silk robe seemed to him a strange garb for a gardener he knew from his experience that it was not well to judge from appearances, so he welcomed the stranger humbly and asked him who these seven young men with him were. The man replied, "These are my new assistants in the Garden." It seemed strange to the Disciple that the new gardener should need so many to assist him in the Garden which for so long he and the Lover had tended alone, but since the man was now his master he did not question the decision but led him round the Garden and showed him all the lovely flowers and beneficial herbs and the butterflies and the bright-colored birds and the nightingale whose note gave such sweetness to the melody of the Garden and the cave of bats and all the other things that were in the Garden and told him all that he knew about the working of the Garden for the pleasure of the Beloved. But the new gardener was silent all the while and at last when they had seen everything and returned to the middle of the Garden he said, "I see that you are an inefficient gardener and have managed the Garden very wastefully."

When the Disciple heard this he was very ashamed that he had been such a bad servant to the Beloved. But the gardener continued, addressing his assistants, "The plants that grow in the Garden are valueless. I will root them out and plant poppy and hemp, tobacco and mandragora, for all of which there is a ready and profitable market, and I will destroy those butterflies whose caterpillars damage the plants. The bright feathers of the birds are of value and marketable but catch that useless brown bird and wring its neck; I will feed no unprofitable mouths. Light a fire and smoke out those loathsome bats and clean out their caves, for I will install in their gloomy and mysterious recesses beautiful maidens who will prove profitable and give men pleasant entertainment."

When he heard this the Disciple said to the man, "Sir, what is this you mean to do? For His creatures which you would destroy are very dear servants of the Beloved and the flowers and beneficial herbs are pleasing to Him."

Then the man's face became the face of a devil and laughing mockingly he replied, "What do I care for the Beloved or His servants or His pleasure? I have deceived you cunningly. The deed and seal were cleverly wrought forgeries whereby I might gain entrance to the Garden to use it for my own profit. The servants of the Beloved are fools and get small rewards for their labors, but the soil of the Garden is rich and much wealth can be made from it."

Then the Disciple answered, "You Deceiver, never while I live will you desecrate the Garden of the Beloved."

Again the Deceiver laughed cruelly and said, "There is no need for you to live, but take my advice and join us in this enterprise, and as you are strong and skilled I will make you second only to myself and you will find it a very profitable venture."

"No," said the Disciple, "I will never do this: seek profit and betray the Beloved."

Therein the Deceiver, losing his patience, became very angry and said to his followers, "Go and seek in the Garden for means whereby I can bring to heel this foolish and obstinate fellow who thus scorns my service and rewards." So his followers went and one of them, opening the gate to the inner Garden, saw the cross and nails and a spear and the crown of thorns, whereupon he returned to the Deceiver and said, "Come and see, I have found implements whereby this felon may die a death worthy of him."

So they seized the Disciple roughly and buffeted him sorely, save only the youngest of the Deceiver's followers, who held back a little until his fellows scoffed at his reluctance and then he too joined them in their violence.

They dragged the Disciple into the inner Garden and tearing off his robe cruelly mocked his nakedness; yet the Disciple was in no way ashamed for it did not seem to him a shameful thing to bear shame for the sake of the Beloved.

Then the Deceiver spoke again to the Disciple: "Change your mind now that you see the doom that awaits you. I am a merciful man and leave my offer open to you if you but agree to submit to my authority. I am very generous in this, for I can still carry out my design whether you help or not."

"No," said the Disciple, "I will never betray the Beloved."

Then the Deceiver laughed more cruelly than ever. "You have betrayed Him already when you handed over His Garden to me."

Then he picked up the crown of thorns and said, "Here is a fitting crown for such a good servant," whereupon he thrust it on his head, not gently as the Lover had once placed it long ago but with such force that it seemed that the thorns pierced even to his brain and the agony that fell upon the Disciple was beyond my pen to describe, yet he had become so inured to pain from the little scratches and galls of the Garden that he did not faint as he had formerly when his agony, compared with this, had been nothing. But he bore all patiently and they took him up and nailed him to the cross and the nails in his hands and feet burned like flames of fire. Then they thrust the spear into his side and I think that there was never in the world greater agony than his.

Yet the agony of his body, although it was the greatest man could bear, was slight compared with the agony of his soul, for he perceived that his sacrifice was wholly in vain and that by his carelessness he had betrayed the Garden of the Beloved to the Deceiver and proved himself an utterly worthless servant, yes and worse, a betrayer of his Lord. And at the same time he had betrayed to death at the hands of the Deceiver his fellow servants in the Garden. For he knew that the Deceiver would tear up the flowers and beneficial herbs which the Beloved loved and plant in the Garden noxious drugs which would be the bane of men. He seemed to see before his eyes the nightingale with its neck broken and the butterflies with their torn wings and all his fellow creatures of the Garden destroyed by his fault, and then it seemed that the torments of his body were far less than his sins deserved. So darkness of body and soul pressed upon him and the taunts of his persecutors sounded in his ears.

Then suddenly he beheld the Beloved.

In the wonder of this vision he forgot all his agony and gazed upon the Beloved with adoration so that his pain became a joy to him. How long he gazed I cannot tell but at last the vision passed.

Yet still a melody of great sweetness sounded in his ears and he looked and beheld the birds of the Garden singing all about him and in the midst of them the nightingale, and the glorious scent of the flowers wafted up to him and he saw that they were bright with butterflies. For the Deceiver and his followers had fled from the Garden overcome by the awful horror of their own crime, save only the youngest of the followers, who knelt at the foot of the cross and seemed to draw strength from gazing at the face of the Disciple. He had thrown away his silken robe and put on the habit of the Disciple, torn and mired as it was from the violence the Disciple had received. Then very carefully the young man drew the nails from the hands and feet of the Disciple and laid him gently on the soft grass, bringing him water to drink and dressing his wounds. Kneeling beside him he said, "Sir, I pray you to teach me this wonderful love of the Beloved."

Then the Disciple was glad, for he heard the voice of the Beloved saying, "Faithful Lover, do this also for the love of Me," but he was so weak as yet he could only whisper "My son."